Letters to a Blind Man

America, God, Love, And Myself

C.J. Dudley

To Becky
Thank you for the support
I appriciate you!!

Print ISBN: 978-1-54393-182-2

eBook ISBN: 978-1-54393-183-9

Table of Contents

Socially Unacceptable

What is Your View 5

State of America 10

Music Vs the Board of Education 12

Divided States of America 13

Coonin 18

Church and State 22

Black in America 24

Black Family 30

Protection of God

You Gave Me 35

Witness 36

Wish I Knew, What I Know 37

When You're Feeling 39

The Punchline 41

Spiritual Fight 43

Sewed Up 45

One Day in April 48

Not Over Yet 50

None of My Business 52

My Struggle 54

Meal Plan 56

Look at God Now 57

Lights On 58

Lift Up My Hands 59

Holding Weight   60

God Got Me   62

Glass House   63

G's Up   65

First Impression   67

First Choice   69

Faith Fanatic   70

Face to Face with Myself   72

Come to Him   74

Circumstances Lie   75

Change in Me   76

In Love with Love

You Used to Love Him   79

Write A Song   81

When the Wind Blows   83

TravelMancing   85

Hands of Time   87

I'm The Kind of Guy You Need   89

I Like the Way   90

I Got It   91

Open Your Heart   92

Thought Process

Words   95

Welcome to My City   97

Treat Me Like   99

That Guy   100

Riding the Fade   101

Where Are the Words   104

Peace and Chaos   106

Number Ones   107

Hustle Like A Boss   109

Drinks Up   111

Built Bad   114

72 Bars   115

My Squad   118

A Letter to My Father   121

A Letter to My Mother   123

Letters to A Blind Man   125

Before I ask you to sit with me
I must be able to sit with myself
Before I ask you to accept my pain
I have to accept the pain myself
Before I ask you to love me
I have to be madly in love with myself

C. Thoth

Introduction

Turning 30 years old, really made me reflect on the previous 12 years of my adult life. I can't lie about the situation, it kind of had me in my feelings, on so many different levels. I was reflecting on some of the situations that I've lived through, experiences that I've had, mistakes that I've made, battles that I've won and lost, being in a place in life, that I never imagined I would be in, and losing and gaining my grip on reality. In the movie *ATL,* T.I. said *"Dreaming is the luxury of children, "* and those words were ringing loud and clear. As a child, I dreamt of recording an album that had the exact same effect as M.J.'s *Thriller* album! I dreamt of having an illustrious movie career! Only accepting the funniest and highest paying offers! I dreamt of going to Berklee College of Music, buying houses for my parents, having a family with my high school sweetheart, having some sort of significant impact on the world. As the ramifications of my life choices started to mold my reality, my childhood dreams were one by one, traded in for bills, drama, and responsibilities. Make no mistake about it, I had *all the time in the world* to pursue any passions that I had, yet, in the mirror stood the reflection of the *best* procrastinator and excuse maker, this side of the Mississippi! So gifted, but no presence! I began to think about what kind of legacy I'm leaving, and I wasn't satisfied with myself. Not that I haven't done *anything* in life, I've released a few studio albums, and I *do* feel like God did with them, what He wanted. But my last full album was in 2010. I decided that my 2010 album was not going to be the finale of my creative dreams and ambitions. I began to write, just expressing my emotions and feeling about things that I've been through, the state of this country, and how God never left my side. Because I was completely honest in every single thing that I wrote, it began to be an organic therapeutic session for me. I was able to be real with myself, and therefore be real with you. Some of my words are subliminal, while others are blatant, but every word is a part of me! So, *read* every word to *understand* me, but *see* every word to *feel* me!

Socially Unacceptable

What is Your View

What does the American flag mean to you?

I ask because I'm coming to realization

That it means different things to different people

I can admit that I was an impressionable child

Because under the government mandated pledge of allegiance in school

I was taught that underneath that flag we all are equal

But as I get older, the truth is

I see the injustice, this flag has no substance

You want my allegiance, but you can't be trusted

I'm distraught and disgusted, minorities get dusted

A broken tail light leads to his chest looking like a hotdog busted

Ran an innocent man down for no reason

There were six cops on that

Snapped his spine in half

Like they were playing Mortal Combat

Triggers get happy, bullets are excited

To pierce the flesh of a black man, and they're hoping we riot

That's when they militarize themselves, and hit the black top

Shells flying everywhere, like they work at the Crab Pot

What, you think I'm playing, look it up on your laptop

A crackhead runs from a lazy cop, so he gave him a back shot

I've seen it with my own eyes, the corruption of law

I'm talking officers, prosecutors, judges and all

They play the game dirty, they're rough and they're raw

I'm talking Tom Brady, texting about deflating the ball

Going to the Super Bowl, and then winning it all

Unnecessary roughness to a defenseless player

Damn, they're not making the call

The courts and precinct work in harmony

At the same damn time

Cop sings unarmed black man a lullaby

Then the chorus comes in, singing the same damn line

The officer is on paid leave, while we gather the info

The forte is coming, we can hear the crescendo

We on the edge of our seats, we're holding hands with our kinfolk

Waiting to see if the choir can reach up to that last note

Then the finale happens

And for a split second there's silence, no clapping

We just cannot fathom

We witnessed what happened, but that somehow got passed them

This little show that they do, and swear is so tight

Is the equivalent to Roseanne Arnold on the mic

BOOOOOO

That concert was terrible, I need a break like a Kit Kat

I want my refund, some reparations, and a kick back

Your presentation was terrible

Intonation was irreparable

How can you be so un-sensible

This is obviously intentional

It must be nigger hunting season, and the badge is your license

You're allowed to hunt deer, rabbits, niggers, and bison's

It's ironic, we're such a threat to you

But you want us to see the best in you

The only difference is our skin tone

We're the same as the rest of you

Yes, I'm upset, I'm pissed at the situation

This country mistreats minorities, but with Trump there's a deliberation

This unstable degenerate, is ACTUALLY President

Can you really say with a straight face, that he's America's best representative

He's spicy like jalapenos, icy like cappuccinos

"We're going to build a wall, to keep out all the Latinos"

And it's going to be YUUUUGE

Let's set aside the fact that these words came from the mouth of one of the dumbest people we have in captivity. Can you imagine an America with no minorities? Think about it….

The U.S. without US, is shaky and hollow

I'm talking 9/11 cover-ups, bobble heads, and gelato

It's the equivalent to you making a homemade taco

But skipping the meat, cheese, sour cream, avocado

Tomato tomato, the mole and Horchata

With us missing, then you're giving up the whole enchilada

The taters the tattas, the salsa and the Cha Cha

Without minorities, you wouldn't know how to Lambada

Excuses are kah kah, repercussions are nah dah

Black bodies dumping faster than a bucket of water

The streets are getting hotter, heating up like it's lava

Black men are targeted, no wonder we ain't got fathers

It started with slavery, and they called us the savages

They stole us, sold us, beat us, leaving families in ravages

Worked them to death, just to build your economy

I know what you're thinking, slavery ended a long time ago, get over it

Settle down homie, just follow me

From 1619 to 1865, it was the law of the land to rule over black lives

Backs look like trees, blacks on their knees

Steal a child from their mother, then demanding their fees

Men, they castrated them

There wasn't nothing they could say to them

If you even gave them the side eye

They'd cock that shotgun and turn your dome to a stadium

From 1865 to 1968, we had Jim Crow and lynch mobs

Corrosion and pinch jobs

Being black was a crime, Black Wall Street got the bomb squad

4 little girls, in a church that exploded

Emmett Till dragged out the river, his beaten body was bloated

It's got to be noted, that this country's eroded

From the inside out, the framework is corroded

In the 80's, the war on drugs destroyed the black fabric

Battering rams tearing down houses, and causing havoc

They drove tanks into houses, to eventually admit they were on the wrong street

"I could've swore this was the house, I saw drug dealers here last week"

Someone's home is reduced to rubble, crumbling under their feet

Meanwhile the Nancy Reagan's smiling in the front seat

Now, my people are getting gunned down

Held up and run down

No, I'm not calling the cops

When they show up, its son down

Hands up, no gun found

My analysis, you're a chump now

If law enforcement is a representation of America

Then I understand why people are voting for Trump now

Kaepernick took a knee, in "the land of the free"

To peacefully speak against injustice

Against people like me

But in order to change the subject

And forget about the truth

They said he disrespected the military

And looked down on the troops

I still don't understand where that came from

He said nothing to that effect

He's actually said the opposite

For the troops he has the utmost respect

But the flag doesn't JUST represent the troops

It represents me too

Which takes me back to my original question

What does the American Flag mean to you

We see the flag differently

Because of the things this country has put us through

You can't expect us to see the same thing

Black folks have a different view

State of America

Blind people are concerned about The Art of the Deal

Democrat or Republican, that's the blue or the red pill

Body gone comatose, you're plugged into the system

They download your information, and you carry out the mission

The world is flooded with alternate facts, so choose your reality

Protect the one percent, or preserve your morality

Bullets flying slow motion, we're shooting back to the basics

Now a Neo Nazi is our chosen one, we're officially in the Matrix

Wars funded by Rockefeller, I'm not talking about Jigga

We're focused on the details, but the picture is bigger

Conditioned to retaliate, when they call you a nigger

They supply the ammunition, execution with triggers

The war on drugs, was really a war on black folk

Hillary pandering to the hood, trying to get her that black vote

The government subsidized the heroin, then gave them a bad dose

The media is breastfeeding, but I don't drink it, I'm lactose

Stop and do your homework, read the schematic

They're diminishing my culture, it's an obvious tactic

It started with Brexit, now it's a Bla-xit

Push us to the back of the bus, where the blacks sit

Trying to ban a whole culture, let me give you a fact check

The U.S. kill people in other countries on the regular

We just haven't been hit back yet

You want to build a wall, with that limited access

But you're the plaque decaying the country, you're the abscess

America's a Native land, they were here from the start of the timeline

America's Natives need a hand, an American lifeline

Dogs set loose on protesters, the media won't give them no primetime

Bulldozing Native land, for an American pipeline

But shhh, there's no such thing as injustice, this country is a sanctuary

Even though we're founded on destroying our adversary

Built up an empire, all for the monetary

Destroy the people and things that you don't want, death or the commissary

Trump is a shrinking sphincter, his administration is a bunch of pricks too

As a matter of fact, no one is escaping this slander

If you voted for Trump, you're a dick too

Music Vs the Board of Education

Music is the heartbeat to the American life

A bridge that crosses over barriers

The universal language that brings cultures together

An organic medication to a wounded spirit

Music is a natural wonder

Wonder gives life to creativity

Creativity gives life to progression

Progression makes the world go round

Music creates excitement, about creating something exciting

Causing focus, energy, and drive

Developing personal pride in your work

Coming up with different ways to reach a goal, outside of the premade box

Music can be intellectually stimulating

Making a child a master of memorization

An on the fly, improvisational genius

And have the discipline of a drill sergeant

Music can pull your heart from your chest, and put it on your sleeve

It can change the course of a day, a year, a life

It can bring you up from your lowest point

And lead you to a higher destination

To be educated in music, is to be educated in life skills

Denying a child their right to creativity, shouldn't our interest

Let the beauty of music cultivate their imaginations

Teach them to be an educated, creative individual

Divided States of America

What I write is like crack to your veins
Let me tell you what the fiends are going to cop next
It's a Sativa laced flow, with a cerebral complex
I write phrases on a high note, like a Cee Lo project
The wisdom is homegrown, in my genome process
I feed off the progress
Think more, and talk less
Write up a query, with an alternate theory, on why the world is so weary
How can we be so heartless
2 Pac said it best, in his lyrical text
We have money for war, but can't feed the poor
Greed is running rampant, all day and all night
Give me, give me, give me, that's what the American life's like
Rather let people die, to make sure your pockets are right
I wonder what you'd do for a Facebook like, and a Klondike
There was two billion dollars spent on this election, TWO BILLION
I mean, seriously
Do you know how many tacos two billion dollars can get you
How much better do you think life in America could be
If we just stop politicking, and power tripping
Grow morals, stop being money driven
And stop keeping food under lock and key
In laymen terms, if you're poor you don't get to eat
You don't get shelter either, go find a spot on the concrete

No not that street, there are stores making money

Not that street either, they have lunch rushes and they don't feed the hungry

Not these blocks, not those 8, or those 12 over there

None of the parks either, but you can't stay here

The payoff doesn't always come, to those who work the hardest

A single mother working 2 jobs, and can only afford a micro studio apartment

The prices are too high, and the wages are too low

The subsidize the rich, then tax it all from the broke

There's enough American pie, everybody can get a slice

Enough forks to go around, everybody can get a bite

Enough plates to serve up, everybody can get right

But there isn't enough room at the table

So, dessert is cancelled for the night

Matter of fact, cancel it for your life, no American Pie for you

We're confiscating all of the cookies and cakes too

We're taking all the donuts and scones, the chocolates and peppermints

All the fruity flavor candies, all the gum and the breath mints

Damn

No treats for a fat kid, it's wrong, it's a tragedy

If being rich gets you treats, the 1% must be America's cavity

But it isn't just "the man" that I'm sticking it to

Because the PEOPLE hold more power, than the people we're giving the power to

But what do we do with it, don't worry I'll wait

Grumble and complain, tune in for the debate

Let the system infiltrate your spirit with hate

Your existence is consumed at an incredible rate

Now they're controlling your thoughts, and you're ready to box

They're making stacks off you fools not connecting the dots

The prison system makes a fortune, crushing builders to rocks

The money ties run deep, now let me thicken the plot

When the time comes, to flip the position of power

You start to bite tongues, you run and hide like a coward

You got your luggage packed up, carry on and a tote

And say you're down for the cause, but it's stupid to vote

Now you're pissing me off, but I'm going to refrain from cursing

But you're making me sick, somebody grab the Robitussin

Black people talking noise, saying they don't respect you

You're ready to throw hands, trying get that respect, dude

But you couldn't care less about who's globally repping you

I hope that you're enjoying what not voting is getting you

But you want to know the thing that's equally as dumb

You screw facing, two facing people that are faking the funk

Somebody voted for Trump

Now, if you openly identify with him, and you feel like that's the right move

I respect that you were honest enough to admit you voted for that fool

But you two facing people

You gave us that one face that said we're in this together

Then voted with that two face, now the country is severed

People complain minorities are always crying about race

But you said something in that booth that you won't say to my face

Why you always lying, why you always lying

Ooooh oh my god, why you always lying

I really didn't believe America had so many hateful individuals

I understand we grew up different, and we have different principles

But if I can quote our own country, we're supposed to be indivisible

Liberty and justice for all, that was the principle

But we're divided like a fraction, the Avengers in Civil War

Severed like an artery, split like a Trump divorce

We're trapped in a horror movie, no need for a sequel

It's sugar against sweet and low, in other words, we're not equal

America is high off itself, I'm talking pipes and roll paper

Slow cooking our own death, no chef and no cater

We even shocking ourselves, no gun, all Taser

Yeah America I'm taking shots at you, all straight with no chaser

America is like a scorned woman going crazy, I hope that you're hearing me right

We need to get her focused, mind, body, and spirit right

Use our head to show her she needs to stay on her toes, like Pilates do

Wait a minute, I said

Use our head to shoulder, she knees to stay on her toes

I just bodied you

When I get to talking real talk, I'm like a battle rapper and a cypher

Venom and a viper, target and a sniper

Gazelle and a tiger, cigar and a lighter

Solid as a rock, flow colder than an iceberg

Just ask, and you might learn

Swerve left, then right turn

I mustache you a question, no beard or sideburn

Why are we so quick to hate each other, so quick to throw down

And we perpetuate the hatred, we're ready to go rounds

You hate me, I hate you, I dare you to step across those bounds

The global playground bully, this is America homie, and it can go down

Isis and Russia, guns, bombs, missiles and NATO

We need to karate kick the hatred, as if we're Kato

Putting actions behind our words, but not forgetting to pray though

That God will intervene, and switch our horns for a halo

With words I'm a wordsmith, word play when word switch

Words are powerful, don't act like your words are worthless

If you structure words a certain way, then they really can get to you

Make you feel all type of things that you would never admit to

Perfectly placed words, can cut you deeper than a slice on the hip, dude

I structure my words like a hurricane

What's that mean

That means when I write, you're going to feel like a cyclone hit you

I'm on a mission, and believe that I'm staying the course

I refuse to muzzle my words, I say it with force

If I said it, then I meant it, don't expect no remorse

I serve it up raw and uncut, like I skipped the plug and went straight to the source

If you're offended by my words, and you think they aren't right

You feel a stirring in your spirit, and you're ready to fight

Just remember I'm an animal, lyrical cannibal

Breaking down anecdotes, believe me I'm nice

The deeper I write, then the higher I fly

I've reached the cruising altitude, bought my ticket through Red Eye

I'm never going to claim to be a "watch what I said" guy

The joints I write are so blunt, if you shake, you'll get a head high

But I'm going to let the clouds settle, let the haze go above you

Hating is overrated, want to say that I love you

So, let's plan for different weather, and stitch up the sever

Divided States of America, let's be united together

Coonin

I write a lot about racism in inequality

I'm sorry I'm not sorry, I don't have a written apology

Because I mean everything I say, whether it be opinion or fact

You want an apology from me because you're in your feelings

Ain't nobody got time for all that

Racism is very present, terrorism over the locals

Hate is running rampant, got America in a choke hold

And I'm not just talking about black against white

Other races are racist too, racism an equal right

But since I been black all my life, I'll stick to the race I know

This isn't about black on white, this is black on black, bro

A race baiter, plus race hater, plus pigmentation of a chocolate flavor

Minis pride and responsibility, respect and civility

Multiplied by ignorance and hostility, divided by untapped ability

Is the square root of a coon

A coon will take real racial tension, to argue our situation is dire

A cop kills a kid, you got that riot desire

White boy calls you a nigga, and you're ready to fire

Facebook status saying that we're meant for something higher

Claim you're fighting the good fight, but complaining you're getting tired

White man holds us back, from what we're trying to acquire

Demand equality, we'll do whatever's required

But the fruits of your labor, suggests you're a liar

What have YOU done for the culture, besides make wack music, and get a pay day

Another shuck and jive don't help us, slave master's done Whip'n Nay Nay

How have you advanced us, what's your contribution

Another ass shaking record, so you deal the culture, mental prostitution

How are you advancing the culture, when a dealer's your resume

Your kids see it all, what you think they're going be one day

Pushing poison in the culture, get your paper by any means

I still can't comprehend the physics of sagging skinny jeans

Brother killing brother, and it don't matter who he's with

You're concerned about your cash flow, get you your chips-n-dip

Now everybody's riding strapped, got the Ruger, extended clip

But be the first one's yelling, yo, the police on some bull shit

A coon who will get on Fox News, and downgrade your heritage

Blow below the waist, crippled us like Nancy Kerrigan

You used to be a model to follow, for the black actress

But now Stacy got a Dash in her name, she off the Black's list

All the rappers bragging about, how they're getting they're doe

How they're the king of the streets, they're getting love from the hoes

How they're moving those bricks, pushing those whips

See a big booty Judy, try to get on them hips

Through all of that fabrication, the fact remaining is this

You're the biggest coons and proud to be it, congratulations you idiots

Perpetuating stereotypical type of behavior

Damaging your culture, but you swear your moves are major

That type of ignorant thinking, is the reason that you robbed bro

I'm a bully in the streets, what do I need a job for

And some of you guys REALLY like that life

And for the life of me, I can't understand

Stupidity calls your name, and you reply on command

If you could get your act together, we could build up a plan

That's how the minority takes over supply and demand

How do we combat cooning

Well…. I'm no expert, but maybe we can start by

Redefining the culture, change up the feel

Exchange our ignorance for pride, that's a hell of a deal

Stop tearing each other down, and start to rebuild

Then we can deregulate the game, and even the playing field

Stop killing each other over pride, girls, money, and wo's

The money comes and goes, but when you kill a soul, all for the bank roll

You're pumped that you got $200, that man's dead bro

Black lives matter, white lives are important

Asian and Native American, Mexican, Muslim, they're all an important assortment

There will only be one time, and one place

When every person, of every race

All believe, the same faith

And that's the date of the rapture, headed to the pearly gates

And that'll be the day, when that commonly used phrase "Only God can judge me" will come into play

But until that day happens, we all share this earth

Why do cultures hate each other, why can't we make it work

Cultural bickering continuously grows, and it swells

But coons help destroy their own culture from the inside, that's a culture consuming itself

As if the odds weren't stacked against us, from day one

A white man kills 9 people, he gets arrested and a Whopper meal

A black man gets killed for being in the toy gun section, holding a toy gun

If anyone is able to make sense of that

Please, see me when I'm done

At the end of the day, we shouldn't have to go that extra mile

To prove anything to anyone

We shouldn't have to be shot 4 times

When we've made it clear that we have a gun permit, and a gun

We shouldn't have to say "Black Lives Matter"

If "All Lives Matter" was a true and honest thing

We shouldn't have to be afraid of dying

When we hear the police sirens ring

On the same token

We don't have to present ourselves as folks to be feared

We don't have to kill each other, just to make a point clear

We don't have to sell drugs, to put money in our pocket

And white people aren't the only ones who don't want to see your draws

Go get a suit, and rock it

I dare you to tell me that your demeanor won't be affected

Baggy jeans and a tall T in an interview, isn't well respected

The point I'm trying to make, is don't give them ammunition

We've already been labeled as thugs, don't let their assumptions come to fruition

Stop destroying your own people, and descending on us like a vulture

Be black, be beautiful, help us strengthen the culture

Church and State

The separation of church and state
Is the separation of person and faith
Laws put into place to tell me what I can and can't say
Schools telling students when they can and can't pray
America is full of people, who all believe differently
So, when it comes to religion and politics, people get a little finicky
But I'm in love with Jesus, so I have to rep the squad
Even if nothing ever comes of it, I STILL rep my God
And to every other religion, Muslim, atheist, and Buddhists
I mean no disrespect, but I'm still going to do this
America needs Jesus, look at the issues
The pain is tear jerking, but God is the tissues
Laws are being made, but what purpose do they serve
The law that man created is kicking God's law to the curb
As if it's outdated, and has no relevance in America
God's cut out the picture, no wonder there's mass hysteria
Some folks say we need more gun laws
Other folks say we don't need guns at all
In my humble opinion, we need God's law
Because it's a known fact, that love makes hate fall
The definition of love is God, and love conquers hate
But if God isn't present, hate grows at a rapid rate
Just take a look around, it's the death of a nation

Laws built up like walls of division and separation

But I guess this was predestined, you can read it in Revelation

That's means rapture is coming soon, I pray Jesus has your registration

Black in America

Black in America, an American black

Not to be confused with an African American

Because I have never been to Africa, nor do I plan on going back

That's no disrespect to my African brothers and sisters

I love you with all my heart

But understand, I was born and raised in Seattle, Washington

So, when labeling me, American is where it starts

Life for a black person in America is never dull and full of action

But if you don't live it, then you don't get it

So, let me break it down like a fraction

Not all black people are hoods and thugs

Not all black people sell and do drugs

Not all black people want to take your purse, ask me what I do for a living, I work

I have a nice office and my desk is dope

But stereotypical undertones make it hard to cope

But I'm an upstanding citizen so I keep my hope

But being black in America, I'm walking a tightrope

Life ain't fair Reaganomics, get ran up on, it's empty pockets

You ain't got nothing on you, he clicks then clock it

You close your eyes, praying that Lord's going to stop it

If I steal on this fool, then I hope he drop it

I might rob him take his hat and wallet

Put it on World Star and I'll make him watch it, wait, wait, wait, wait, wait, stop it

It's back to reality I'm back on the scene

Everything that just happened was all in daydream

Except the gun still present, the dude is still mean

Honestly, it's taking everything not to scream

I ain't a thug, I ain't a gangster, I just got caught slipping

But if this is how I die, then Lord please forgive him

But then I see 1Time blow up the spot

I've never been so happy in my life to see a cop

Then the dude gets spooked and he drops his Glock

He took off down the alley and he circled the block

I said ayo police, wave my hand in the air

Dude just tried to rob me, and he ran down there

Then the cop swerved up and he jumped out the coop

Pulled the heat out and said hands up or I'll shoot

WO!!!!

Now I'm really trippin I don't know what to do

But I put my hands up because mama ain't raise no fool

Don't shoot officer, I committed no crimes

Man, I'm so sick and tired of you thugs and your lines

Say one more word and I'll put five in your gut

Now get on the ground and keep your mouth shut

All you thugs think your slick, now what set are you reppin

You're on the wrong side of town with an illegal weapon

Yo you got it all wrong man, that ain't my gun

Why do you think I waved you down and chose not to run

He put his knee in my back, slapped on the cuffs

Forearm around my neck and now he's choking me up

Now my breath is getting short and I'm losing my vision

Then he cracks me over the head and said stop resisting

I can see the people panicking, ain't coming to get me though

But everybody's got a phone out taking a video

Is this how I die by a cop that so smug, honestly, I prefer being shot by a thug

Politicians and police all standing in unity

One less black man means a better community

They get a paid vacay and granted immunity

And you wonder why black folks riot and mutiny

Flash back to the 50's I'm bringing it up

When they were torching black folk and they were stringing them up

When the KKK was patrolling at night

Looking for a black face they can smash with a pipe

I'm talking kids, pre-teens, young adults and old people

All we ever wanted was the chance to be equal

Hit them with the civil rights, boy we swerved on'em

Political response, hoses turned on'em

Can't use the same bathroom or drink the same water

Get attacked at the lunch counter placing an order

To the back of the bus got to stay in your place

Disrespect a white person and vanish without a trace

We shall overcome is the song that we sing

Until America showed us how to murder a King

With no rights and no hope, you wonder what's next

Get your hand out their pocket while they cross out an X

Seems the government's content with having local enemies

And when they tried to do right they even snuffed out the Kennedy's

Man.... seems like the law ain't nothing more than

White thugs with black slugs, with a clip in the steel Mac

I'm amazed that Obama's cap ain't been peeled back

We hungry for justice, boy we stay starvin

Skittles and iced tea, that's Trayvon Martin

You want to buy a cigarette don't ask me partner

Because I can't breathe, and that's Eric Garner

Who's gonna get popped next, it's the roll of the dice

I'd avoid swing sets, or end up like Tamir Rice

They say it's part of the job, but it's more we all know

And don't drop your wallet, Amadou Diallo

Oh, the list goes on, I'll continue the countdown

Dontre Hamilton, John Crawford, Ezell Ford, and Mike Brown

Sandra Bland, Tanisha Anderson, this just ain't right

Michael Ealy, Tony Robinson, Akai Gurley, and Phillip White

Tamir was a 12-year-old black kid in a park

And he took one to the chest

But a grown white man kills 9 black people at church

And they give him Burger King and a bulletproof vest

Now let the media tell it, 9 black people were slain

I find that disrespectful, because 1 of those 9 has a Senator in front of his name

I don't know, to me that seems like an attack on the judicial

I mean, you know…. knocking off a state official

If the roles were reversed, and the shooter was black

They would've made that fool head-butt a missile

But to the contrary, the police were very nice and civil

Why is it that dealing with black people never seems that simple

When will it end, when is the victory won

American politics is built so that nothing ever gets done

So, here's what I think, I'm going to shed a little light

What you're doing isn't working, so something new won't hurt right

Where does it end, it ends where it starts

But like Marshawn Lynch, no one wants to tackle this beast, too many moving parts

Just by bringing it up, some folks will break on it

But you won't kill my vibe, here's my take on it

The attack is physical, but the root is spiritual

And if you don't kill the roots first, then any progress is minimal

You have the folks who are cynical, some analytical

I know that you're critical, but let me make it literal

It's like when you cut down a tree, you get a better view

You're seeing things differently, and dare to say it's brand new

But in a couple years that tree starts to grow

But it's not in your view yet, so you don't even know

Then one day you look up, and the tree full grew

Then you say oh, we forgot to pull the roots

See, the roots run deep, and they don't be playing

If you never dig them up, you better believe that they're staying

Imagine what it'd be like if we all start praying

Instead of each other, it would be the demons we're slaying

We're buried under sin, like the bass under treble

When you're buried, how are you supposed to rise to a new level

We need to follow Jesus, but we follow the devil

It's like we really know that fool on a personal level

See we all need Jesus, but a lot are taking Satan

You can roll your eyes if you want to, but you know what I'm saying

If we all had Jesus, then we'd have the love in our hearts

And that how you win the war on hate, before it starts

Just to clarify….

This isn't an I hate whites poem

This is an I need rights poem

This isn't an I hate cops poem

This is a when will it stop poem

A taking the truth from the bottom to the top poem

A stop following Satan, and head towards the Rock poem

It's a stop doing wrong poem

You can even call it a Rodney King, why can't we all just get along poem

Being black in America, it comes with a lot of stress

Is it fair, no, is it reality, yes

So how do I choose to respond in the midst of the ignorance

Simply by saying, God Bless

Black Family

Less daddy's, more fathers

Less ho's, more mothers

Less brawd's, more sisters

Less nigga's, more brothers

Hell of a way to start a conversation, I realize

But real eyes, realize, real lies

And from what I see, this lie is on the loose

It's time to run it down, need to strap up your boots

Because this lie is running deep, I'm talking down to the roots

We're convinced that the lie IS a lie, it's like we lie in cahoots

What ever happened to the strong black family, the strong black unity

The strong black role models, who live in the strong black community

What ever happened to the strong black father, who ACTUALLY raised his kids

Help his daughter with her homework, then gave her a math quiz

Be at his son's every practice, take him to the park and play with him

Teach how to be a man, and how to treat women

Take his kids out to lunch, go to the beach when you're done

Daddy daughter dates, football games with his son

Eat breakfast with them every morning, and dinner every night

You check under the bed to reassure them, that everything is alright

And before you tuck them into the bed where they lay

Tell me what happened to the father's that pray

What ever happened to the strong black mother, who never gives up

When her kids are going crazy, she's steady lifting them up

What ever happened to PTA meetings, helping with bake sales, and all

That comforting voice for your son, when he falls

What ever happened to art projects at night, just to spend time with your baby

Making home cooked meals, no time to be lazy

Pack your kids lunch and you send them to school

With a note in their lunch that says I love you, PS don't go up in there acting like a fool

The strong black mother, who's all work and no play

Tell me what happened to the mother's that pray

Whatever happened to young black brothers, who spoke intelligently

Move with a purpose, and walk with integrity

His wardrobe didn't make him, his shoes didn't break him

He put the "student" in student athlete, got that college education

Working two jobs, determined to succeed

Didn't blow his money on rims, women, and weed

A strong black man, lending a helping hand to the weak

Drops what he's doing to help the elderly cross the street

He knew the world was a lot bigger than the neighborhood he repped

Chased knowledge, not ignorance, he watched where he stepped

A classy young man, always ready to take on the day

Tell me what happened to brothers that pray

Whatever happened to strong black sisters, who's mind defined her

Not her hairstyle, sex appeal, or wardrobe designer

The sister who knew her worth wasn't wrapped up in a man

She wasn't digging for gold, because she has her own plan

It was never her goal to be in the Bad Girls Club

Successful men caught her attention, not the likes of a scrub

Walked with boldness, and was proud, independently she stood

Worked her way up to CEO, but never forgot the hood

Her mere presence kills, and her intelligence slay

Tell me what happened to the sisters that pray

Protection of God

You Gave Me

You gave me the strength

To climb the highest mountain

You gave me the patience

To praise you when the battle's not over

You gave me a new life

You took away my pain and sorrow

You gave me a clean heart

How can I ever repay you

I give you my heart, I give you my all

I give you my ear, so I can hear when you call

I give you my thanks, I can't say it enough

Thank you for never giving up on me

Witness

Silence takes over
I fall down on my knees and pray
A silent, agonizing cry is all I can muster
I wish I had more to say
Life isn't easy
Close friends are few
Standing alone in a crowded room
Crying out to you
The devil is a liar
My God is in the blessing business
The world says to keep it to yourself
But I am called to be a witness
So, I tell it, my story
Well, I'm telling at least a part
You've witnessed the transformation of a man
It all started with Jesus touching my heart

Wish I Knew, What I Know

I almost gave up, when the darkness came

I was feeling so low

I didn't know what to do, I didn't know how to be

I didn't know where to go

I started doing things that I never did before

I started going places that I said I would never go

I started thinking things that scared me

I can't thank you enough, Lord you were there for me

Pulled the knife back, watched the blood drip

Tears streaming down my face

I hear your voice, saying don't quit

I don't feel like I'm in proper shape to finish this race

Feels like more than I can bare, and it's only getting harder

Confused because I feel I've gone too far, simultaneously feeling too weak to go further

But I know I don't have to do this alone, Lord your Word is perfection

You're always there to shelter me with your loving arms of protection

Every day was dark, I had a cold heart

Chills were running through my veins

When you looked at me, I made sure you couldn't see

All my hurt and pain

I don't know why I did it, thought I could hide with it

But my God knows all

Praise the Lord for never hanging up on me

And continued to call

I wish I knew then, what I know now

I probably wouldn't be, where I am now

But I know now, what I didn't, then

And I'm changed now, I'm a different man

When You're Feeling

There are times in everyone's life, when it gets hard

And it feels like you can't go on

You say I used to be strong, but now I'm not

And I feel like I can't hold on

When I have them days, that I don't feel like getting out of my bed

Because nothing good is waiting for me

I know that life goes on, but it's so hard

Because I don't feel like I have what I need

Can't take my mind off of everything that I've been through

Racking my brain about what I should do

This isn't cool

And I am feeling so alone

Hard to go to sleep because I'm stressing out

I want it to get better, but I got my doubts

Help me out

Lord I'm feeling so alone

When you're feeling weary

And you feel like you don't know what to do

Just call on the name of Jesus

He'll step right in and carry you

Nothing's too big for the Father

Not even a heart that's full of pain

I know because He did me

Touched my heart and took my pain away

When you're feeling lonely, when you're feeling down hearted

Look to Jesus because He's always there

The Punchline

God's word is uncompromising, makes my flow mystifying

Known for being a singer, but now my flow is hypnotizing

Got you thinking, what's the reason, change of season, boy it's treason

Leave the rapping to the pros, I think it's best you stick to singing

You don't like my flow, turn your station off

John Travolta, Nicolas Cage, me and the devil are Facing Off

The love of God is like Ben Button, the Case is Curious

The devil got mad real quick, Fast and Furious

The devil says to Get Shorty, DeVito, I'm standing tall on the word of God, so we know

He really thinks his tricks are iron hard, Magneto, but I Marvel at Jesus the X factor, hero

If you're with devil in the end, you're going to feel the Major Payne

Feeling so dumb, use your Pinky scratch your Brain

The world as a whole is in denial, look around Americans, too many Idols

I think it's best you tell the devil, Deuces,

And read God's Graffiti or catch the devil's Exclusives

Out there steady making trouble, with Vinny, your Cousin

The devil sells you sin, because they're Cheaper by The Dozen

Pull a straight G. I. Jane, and keep your head buzzing

God made my flow sick, someone get the Robitussin

Give my all to God, He's my source of motivation

Flow getting grimy like Garfield, before the renovation

You need to get saved right now, because time's flying

God already paid the cost, at the cross, no need to Get Rich or Die Trying

It's Bizarre, the devil's a Kon Artist too, I'm not spitting Eminems, he's Kuniving, here's the Proof

Really? The Big Bang Theory, that's a muddy gesture, read the Word of God, you're acting real Nutty Professor

You need to walk with God and stay in compliance

Then you'll have no problems when you're Facing the Giants

I been through the test, and I came out a changed man

Showed the Lord my deck of cards, and He made it Rain Man

So, I give my praise to God, because the Lord is glorious

The devil thinks he's B.I.G., but he's Notorious

Those other gods are fake, man, don't deny the truth

I'm like the Hebrew boys, my faith is Fireproof

Steady in my Word, because I have to get to writing

Don't ball up my fist no more, Jesus does my fighting

Want to know more about Jesus, then please let me enlighten

He's smoother than Michael Jackson was, before the light skin

Serve you up a plate of God's Word, go head and eat it

Speaking from experience, I know we all need it

The Word of God will stand forever, never be defeated

Not like Super Bowl 40, when Seattle was cheated

Alright that's about it, enough of the games

Slam dunk the Word of God in your face, King James

Spiritual Fight

Terrorism doesn't scare me, I'm not concerned about Isis

I have my own worries, my own personal crisis

I'm in the midst of a war against the devil's devices

Just the other day, I took a Holy Ghost bomb, shoved it down the devil's throat

And blew that demon into several slices

I'm a little graphic with the vernacular

But that's how an ordinary story becomes spectacular

America's got a heart problem, that's cardiovascular

The devil appears and disappears like smoke, it's a silent massacre

He moves in the shadows, feeding off spiritual death

We don't have time to be silent, or mumbling under our breath

It's time to call those spirits by name, whether it be fornication or jealously

Or hate, or a wicked tongue, maybe you're imbalanced chemically

Maybe it's greed you struggle with, or maybe pride is your issue

Call that spirit by name, then slice its head off with a Ginsu

Decapitating spirits that are locking you up in bondage

The word of God is the sword, when you swing it, you're slinging knowledge

Demons on the hunt, they're looking and trying to find me

Put the struggle in my face, thinking they're going to blind me

But I've been through the fire, and Jesus said he refined me

The devil's got nothing on the legion that's behind me

The devil's trying to do me, and trying to put me in lies again

Trying to get me out of my zone, anger is on the rise again

But I stare the devil in the face, and I get to sizing him

Then I cross him up, like they're calling me Alan Iverson

I've got my sword drawn and I'm ready for war

And I'm led by the spirit, that's what I follow Him for

Narrow road, I stay steady

Weapons hot, I stay ready

I got the sword and the shield, like a buccaneer

I get to cutting demons up in here, like a musketeer

Because the presence of God will make a demon run in fear

Have him running up Mt Rainier, like he was a mountaineer

But action gets thick, I'm feeling weaker and weaker

Lord it's hard to hear your voice, can you turn up the speaker

I know you didn't leave me, I'm a strong believer

Please bless me with your strength, I'm a willing receiver

Then I retreat to my war room, so no one can find me

I slam the door shut and I lock it behind me

Then I fall to my knees, praying to God, please

Make me bold, don't let me freeze, Lord please put my mind at ease

Then I hear the Lord's voice, He's shedding some light for me

He said relax in His spirit, He's about to fight for me

I continue to pray, I feel it, I'm getting stronger

But I'm going to keep praying, just a little bit longer

When God says to pray, pray is what you do

When He says get on the good foot, that means it's time to move

When He says pull out the sword, that means the Word is coming through

I said all of that, to say this

And when Jesus died for my sins, He died for yours too

Sewed Up

The Lord knows that I can get in a cycle

I'm backsliding, moonwalking like I'm Michael

I'm really tripping, my game is slipping

It really shows

Walk up in the church, fall on my face

I'm screaming help me Lord

People look concerned and they're tapping me on the hip, bro

Why am I running back to Jesus, and what it hit for

Smoking a lot of loud, but I'm keeping it on the low though

Life is picture perfect, just take a look at the centerfold

This is what I wanted dog, money, girls, expensive cars

But my goals in life are changing, I'm racing, I'm chasing after God

But things are moving so fast, I need to get my mind right

I've grown accustomed to customizing the limelight

It's not about me, I'm stealing credit, it's such a crime

Step up on the stage, I lose my mind, they call me prime time

I can't lie, I love the attention my talent gets me

Do a show, get my money, take a cutie with me

A game that little kids play, but now I'm responsible

Call me Professor X, because I got that mind control

Let it sink in, let the flavor marinate

I know what you're thinking, no need for me to interrogate

Beyoncé's not the only one who has a glass of lemonade

Take a sip, while I spit

Now back to the serenade

Switch up how I walk, and update my vernacular

I'm an ordinary man, but God is spectacular

So, I may never know, what it feels to be like you

He's got Glock in his Rarri, I have a car seat in my van

I'm making plans, doing deals for grands

Shaking hands, savage on the microphone

Fans screaming, he's the man

Because I do this, don't misconstrue this

But I got the feeling that I turn my back on Jesus

Like my name was Judas

I thought I was the coolest, but I'm really acting foolish

Last thing I want is to get to Jesus, and He says who's this

So, I hit a U-y, I tell you truly

I'm coming back to the battlefield, guns out, call of duty

One eye closed when I aim, bout to let it pop

They say I'm acting petty

That's why they call me Petty Wap

Now I'm back on my grind, it took a little time

Life was on fast forward, but Jesus just hit rewind

Until the day I die, I'm always repping mine

So, I may never know, what it feels to be like you

Of course, I think she's fine

But I've got God on, my mind

And that's no shade on her behind

But I'll tell you one more time

That for God I'm sewed up

And I'm so glad He showed up

I'm young guy, in God I trust

Having Jesus is so clutch

Yeah baby

One Day in April

Why can't I just fucking die

My life is shit, I'm messing up other people's lives too

It's my own selfishness that's causing me to continuously make things worse

I'm a grown man, I make the decisions to do what I do

And there is absolutely no excuse for it

But why do I do it

Here I am again, back in a fucked-up situation that I have nobody to blame but myself

Now I'm in this basement, using a Swiss army knife to carve lines in my arm

For some stupid fucking reason, I think that if I die

It will all be ok

I'll stop fucking up, everyone can go on their merry way

And it will all be good

It's one thing if I screw up my life, but I really don't want to mess anyone else up in the process

Yet, I can't seem to master the art of screwing myself without dragging other people into it

The shit is not fair, what do I do

I just want to be fucking normal

How did I get here

I hate myself, I hate what I represent

And what I represent is my own dumb ass

Why the hell am here

To preach, what can I even preach about anymore

I'm a liar, a hypocrite, and a fornicator

I have nothing good and useful to say to anyone anymore

Concerning the word of God

I have released 2 studio albums, a live album, and a mix tape

All preaching the word of God

If those albums are going to be my legacy, then why the hell am I not dead yet

What more could I possibly do, that will be effective in the Kingdom of God

Pacing around this room like a fucking maniac

Knife in hand, stopping to write a few words

Create another jagged edge on my arm, then back to pacing

Trying to make sense of a senseless life

Not Over Yet

I have to be honest, need to keep it funky

Living life as a Christian gets a little bumpy

People make their own plans, that's a given

But it's different when you're trying to live as a Christian

I really try to walk the talk, it's hard though

Trying to cruise through life, but my car broke

But I made up in my mind, that there's no tomorrow

I'm done going down to the wire, Marlo

I feel like my mission is something people should get behind

I'm building a regiment, all my soldiers get in line

But I don't need any cowards, to roll with me, you need a spine

Ain't a squad in the world, that's will be as tough as mine

Study and praying, singing and hanging, is what we do

Lifting each other up, because I need prayer just as much as you

Headed to the battlefield, with my sword and shield too

Fighting on my knees, while we're praying in the war room

The war isn't over, it's intermission though

New evidence has surfaced, you can see the video

Bombs and missile and terrorist are really tripping, yo

Protesting every day, like we're in the 60's, bro

And if you're paying attention, then you notice the tension

America's about the greed, not the competition

The game is rigged, and they really don't expect you to fight

But I got a plan, introducing Jesus Christ

And my plan is to have a crew on the front row

Praying for the nation, and praying that Donald Trump goes

I pray you forgive us, for every time a bomb blow

Trump supporters all can get a piece of this combo

Know that I got love for you, I pray that God touches you

I'm standing in the gap, just in case He feels like crushing you

I choose to follow God, if you don't, then you will be wrong

It's a war zone, choose which side you will be on

None of My Business

I find it interesting
The way my mind breaks things down, metaphorically
If I got a question, don't assume that I'm rhetorically
Asking because I got a preconceived notion
Going through the motions, just so I respond accordingly
They say my arrogance precedes me, haters don't believe me
But I study for myself, I don't swallow what they feed me
You got a brain, so use it, come to your own conclusion
Believe what you want to, that's your right as a human
But spiritual ethic, you deny and discredit
A political view on religion will send you to hell if you let it
But I understand
Because there's certain things you can't shake me on, so don't even try
As for me and my house, some things just don't fly
I equate it to a bird on the 4th of July
I'm setting bombs off, watch me knock these crows out the sky
Jesus paid it all, point, blank, and period
You really want to argue about this, man, are you serious
If you don't want to hear it, that's cool, at least I told you
I don't want to argue, I'll brush the dirt off my shoulder
Continue on my mission, because my journey's not over
Japan to Costa Rica, Australia to Nova Scotia
Front line on the battlefield, I'm a soldier
I'm rolling with the Rock, so naturally I get boulder

Cold cold world, and sin is making it colder

That's why I'm on a mission, preaching the same word I told you

But like I said, if you don't want to hear it, hey, I'm not tripping on you

Who knows, in the future God might flip it on you

It's not my job to beat you over the head homie

Go on and live your life, the best way that you can homie

How you live your life, it's not for me to judge

But as for me and what I believe, I'm not going to budge

Because I believe

Heaven is for real, paradise for the soul

The purely gate's my finish line, my ultimate goal

I can't wait for the day I walk the streets of gold

Walking next to the Lord, and my hand He will hold

I hope He shows me around, get a feel for the town

Go and hear the angels sing, man that choir gets down

The praise party don't stop in Heaven, they get it popping

And it goes harder than Michael Jackson with Thriller dropping

You're eternally in the presence of God with no fears

No sickness, no arguing, no death, and no tears

But I also believe

Hell is as real, as a weapon concealed

You may not see it tucked away, but you feel the burn of the steel

Not a speck of light in sight, the darkness takes on a feel

You're tearing at your own flesh, and you're feeling it peel

Negotiating with the darkness, trying to cut you a deal

Screaming God please listen, I'm willing to do your will

See you knew in the beginning, that Jesus, He paid the bill

But you chose not to serve Him, your decision was ill

But…. that ain't none of my business

My Struggle

Last night I tried to kill myself

Put the knife to my wrist, dragged it slow

Watched my skin, as it split

I didn't bleed enough, adding to my stress level

Six separate slices, all of them were unsuccessful

If I had a gun, I might've popped one

My daddy crying, thank God you ain't got one

If I had a thick rope, and I had the height

I would've tied a necktie knot, then I'd take a flight

You ever felt like you were locked up, but not in prison

Like you can't enjoy a gift that you were freely given

Like you were sent to war, but without a mission

You can't grab your gun to shoot because your holster's missing

Like staying up all night to study for a test

Just to find out in the morning that you read the wrong text

It was a snowball effect, everything was crumbling

My fall was so deep, I can't even call it stumbling

Landslide, flood water, thunder, and the lightning flash

Marriage going down the toilet, life is going in the trash

Money going down the drain, living life with no cash

Living out of my truck, I'm paying rent, but you call it gas

Fast forward down the line, just a couple months

Insomnia setting in, I can't even sleep without a blunt

Every night, going to my sister's, and I'd turn up

Take a bottle to the head, call a chick, and burn up

I ignored my feelings, hid the pain, suppressed the hurt

Once a funny outgoing guy, now an introvert

Smile gone, I don't talk, people saying what's the deal

Maybe I don't want the world to know exactly how I feel

Yeah, I went to counseling, it helped for a minute, man

But hearing everybody's story, I'm more depressed than when I came

Driving around town, trying to find the right spot

Park the hooptie, go to sleep, don't want no drama from the cops

Sleeping in the front seat, wake up, then I go to work

Got to keep my jacket on, because I couldn't clean my shirt

There's no toilet in my truck, so my stomach really hurt

I wash up at the sink in the bathroom when I get to work

Through all of the pain and embarrassment, let me tell you what's left

Had to take this opportunity to get it off my chest

Praying on my knees, asking Precious Lord, what's next

This darkness won't last forever, I know I'm going to pass this test

Lord I want to thank you for the job that you gave me

I'm sorry that I got a little lazy, a little shaky

But I praise you Lord, because from the knife you saved me

Times are hard, but I'm harder, Lord that's how you made me

I know I have a purpose, and I'm coming to fulfill that

Ain't no situation in the world going to kill that

Ten months, two car crashes tried to peel me back

God is my protection, I'm still standing, you feel that

Moral of the story is that life's going to happen

Choose how you will respond, with your words and your actions

I started off rough, but I'm going to see the race through

So, for the good, the bad, and the ugly, I say thank you

Meal Plan

Trials and tribulations, it got my mind racing

Looking for a better day to come, anticipating

Lord I'm so sick of waiting, you're improving my patience

But everybody's on that "you can't do that," why they hating

And Lord, the hate is blatant, and my angers inflating

I wish they'd take a fade away shot, Gary Payton

My situation, hate it, but I know I can make it

Lord I'm traveling your path, on my way to greatness

There's so many people that I need to preach to

So many situations that you need to reach through

I give you straight talk, make sure you know the deal

Yeah, they call me preacher man, because I keep it real

I'm an open book, I tell you how I feel

God's Word is my food, time for a meal

Look at God Now

For the longest time, I felt like I was going in circles

And I felt like it would never end

I would start in one spot, then journey forever

But end up in the places that I've already been

I said this looks familiar, I think I've been here before

But I can't seem to get away

I'm walking into a wall, Lord please open the door

And let me see the dawn of another day

Lord I know you never let me down, and you'll never lead me astray

I know it's only for a season

I know you will never put more on me than I can bare

And I know you have your reasons

Fire refines gold, pressure produces diamonds

I can't wait to see what you do

Change me from the inside out

I entrust my life to you

Look at God now, look at what He's doing

Hear what He is saying, it's so exciting

Look at God now, He's doing a new thing in me

Lights On

When the music fades
And nothing is left on stage, but me
When the band goes home, and the lights go out
And it's too dark to see
The only thing left are my thoughts
And they begin to carry me
Do I really have what it takes to soldier on
The question of the hour is, what's wrong
There's too much in the atmosphere, I need to slow it down
For the battle isn't mine, Lord I need you now
I try to pick my battles, swing blindly into the night
It's hard to differentiate what's wrong, from what's right
Doing this on my own, I consistently fail
My life's tank is on empty, I need a refill
Lord fill me back up, I want to stop playing
Teach me to lean on you, and remind me to keep praying
Life doesn't stop when I walk off the stage
The street is the real battlefield, and it's a war that I'll wage
My mission is clear, and I wasn't built for prudence
I'm a teacher of the gospel, and the streets are my students

Lift Up My Hands

When I feel alone
When I feel no one cares
And the raindrops fall over me
When there's nothing left
Inside of me to give
Except the tears that flow
The Lord said
Take a look at your life
From way back when, till now
Jesus is the only way out
I lift up my hands, and I pray that
You'll give me the strength to stand, and I hope that
Tomorrow is a brighter day, and I give my life
Give it to you all the way

Holding Weight

When you talk about a name that holds weight

You're talking about something important

It could be a kingpin, it could be a celebrity

Or the name on a ballot voting

Gloating and showboating about your name, and how you're a boss

But your name doesn't hold the same weight as the name of the man who carried that cross

And it's certain, put the work in, cut the curtain

Jesus body was mangled

Beat him with the chain, beat him with a whip

Put him on the cross, and they put him in an upward angle

Treason's the reason for teasing, seeming they won't be believing

Season for reaping is creeping, I see you starving, we're eating

You think it's odd, but it's even, pride got you turning and leaving

Sin in your soul and it's leaking, leading the souls that are grieving

They let Barabbas free and, put the cuffs on Jesus' hand

Put him in the town square, and people watched them beat this man

Bleeding out the head because he got thorns in it

I couldn't take the pain for more than 4 minutes

If it was up to me, I'd have been forfeited

But that's why his name holds weight, because He didn't

Hit him with the slow death, put him in the tomb

Rock in the doorway, locking up the room

But you can see it on paper, three days later

See him walking around, with a smile like hi hater

Death can't hold him, and the devil can't stop him

Living life without him, and it's going to be a problem

You ain't a boss, take a loss, baby don't hate

And that's why the name of Jesus is holding that weight

Jesus never quit, never gave up the fight

Sacrificed His perfect body, just to save our life

You want to get to Heaven, then give Him your soul

Now you officially know the weight His name holds

The name of Jesus, is holding weight homie

That's how you get to Heaven, make no mistake homie

At the pearly gates, He'll be judging souls

Now you officially know the weight His name holds

God Got Me

I've been around the block, time or two

I've been through some things, that I wish I never been through

I've seen some dark things, and I've seen darker things then that

Gone so deep down the wrong road, I thought I would never get back

I've been to the highest high, and to the lowest low

God gave me a testimony, so I have to let you know

I've had them days I cried all night

I've had them nights I cried all day

But Jesus told me that He'd never

No, no never leave me

Nor forsake me, so I'm standing on His holy word

Glass House

There's of couple things I want to say, and even more things that I won't

There's a few things I need to say, and even more things I don't

Being me can fun, because my swag is on fleek

Being me can be exciting, because I march to my own beat

Even though I'm fat, being me, you feel sleek

But being me is dangerous, because being me, ain't for the weak

Everything that I've tried to be, plus everything that I'm called to be

Plus, everything that I've grown to be, mixed with everything that you've thrown at me

Add in the man that I claim to be, plus the man I'm portrayed to be

Plus, the man I was made to be, plus the man I'm afraid to be

DAMN

Seems like I have more personalities than a schizo on Pop Rocks

I tell you how I really feel, like a rerun of The Boon Docks

Yet my moves stay smooth, like MJ on a pop lock

Sometimes I wish I could fly, Nutso on the roof top

Four-inch blade making slices, cold cut

Even on sunny days, I see the clouds, roll up

Wish I could go back in time, no such luck

You don't like me, I don't give a fuck and so what

Of course, that's just the exterior, the interior isn't the same

It's like my feelings are the picture, and my actions are the frame

I've made some money, had some girls, even had a taste of fame

Looking back on all I've been through, I wonder if I'm crazier than what I claim

But at the end of the day, this life is my own

I don't have to answer to you, I barely answer my phone

I answer to God, and he's got a lot of work

On Sunday, the pastor's spitting the truth and it hurts

But it's a pain that can heal me, a pain that can build me

I let you see the struggle, in hopes that you feel me

I don't quit, I don't leave, I got no time for goodbye

If I always quit when it gets hard, I'd never get anywhere, would I

It's like the first 57 minutes of the NFC Championship

The situation was a real son

But I don't quit in the last 3 minutes, I GOT WIL-SON!!!

G's Up

Comparing little g to big G, that's like...

Flag football to rugby

Fresh and clean to muddy

3-piece suit to grungy

Feeling good to feeling crunchy

Being broke to having money

Cloudy days to being sunny

A corny dude to being funny

That's like a lion to a bunny

No rhythm to being funky

A smooth ride to being bumpy

Being full to being hungry

Being beautiful to being ugly

There's only one true G, the rest all lied

Big G sent His son, and on the cross is where He died

3 days later He stepped out of the tomb

Sweeping up sin, dust pan and a broom

Little g's can't hang, they can't handle the business

Big G is like Popeye, coming straight off the spinach

Grown man to a child, bold to timid

LOB to NFL, man they scared to scrimmage

A bus to a Ferrari, grown woman to a Barbie

Jurassic Park to Barney, Xbox live to Atari

Can't win to can't lose, a rowboat to a cruise

Fresh J's to Shaq Fu's, Fox Network to news

They're not the same thing, check the bells, His name rings

Marciano to Louis, it's the opening ding

Brick to iPhone, desktop to a tablet

Promoting on Facebook verses signed and established

A mud puddle to the ocean, spit to lotion

A V Dub bug to a 6-4, hitting the 3-wheel motion

A dead end to a highway, the wrong way to the right way

I praise God the Father, whatever He say, I say

He's coming back and it's lethal, wherever He go, we go

LeBron James dunk compared to Shaq with a free throw

Little g's not working, big G's going ham

Tuna fish to sushi, filet mignon to spam

I roll with big G, and we roll tough

Now you know what I mean when I say G's up

First Impression

Like any human being, I have limits that get tested

Not every first impression is an impression that's impressive

My words can get excessive, my tone can be oppressive

If you catch me on the wrong day, my hands might get aggressive

I got pain and I be stressing, some people need to learn a lesson

Coming against me, you better up your aggression

All you see is an angry black man, and you're feeling some bad vibes

But you're the one who walked into my proximity's landmines

Of course.... that doesn't define me, but it does remind me

I'm a work in progress, I have to put the past behind me

I'm not what I used to be, but I'm not what I want to be

I'm curious myself, to see what I'm eventually going be

People say I changed on them, now I'm too real on them

Forget about the change, I hundred dollar billed on them

I used to be words without action, or action without words

Now I'm putting in work, while I conjugate verbs

I tell my truth, the way that I see it, if you don't like it, don't read it

Apparently, I speak with an arrogance, that some call conceited

But my words are black and white, like Michael Jackson, you can Beat It

But before you make your mind up, that I'm a menace to society

Detox your assumptions, and listen with sobriety

I know God got me, I don't always have to run my mouth

Victory is in Jesus, I don't have to stomp them out

Learning to unlearn, is an underestimated battle

It's easier said than done, to get back up in the saddle

Learning new ways to tread the water, without a boat or a paddle

To simply stand on the word of God, and not shake or rattle

To slip and lose my footing, is too easy for the kid

Black ice on an incline, the definition of back slid

But I take a deep breath, I grit my teeth

Brush myself off and I stand to my feet

But that's not my final destination, I have to take one more step

Back onto the word of God, and may we never forget

That the ultimate goal, is not to go with the flow

What kind of legacy are you leaving, when you're a professional ho

Or the neighborhood dope man, slanging the dro

When you die, I guarantee you can't take none of your doe

It's not tearing the club up, or throwing them thangs

It's not a mansion on the beach, with a Lac and a Range

It's not about men showing dominance, or women showing prominence

You keep that to yourself, that's why it's called self confidence

It's not about proving you're a boss, because the truth is you're not

And if you die in that sin, you'll be like Mims, screaming THIS IS WHY I'M HOT

But the ultimate goal, is to win and save souls

Because when we cross deaths bridge, we're going to be paying a toll

When you get to the pearly gate, there's going to be a division

Either your name is in the book of life, or it isn't

And by then it's too late to fix, you got fear in your mind

So, I suggest you get it right, while you still have time

First Choice

Lord I know that your love will be

Right here and you'll always care for me

You've always been the one, and I know that it's true

That can't nobody love me the way that you do

I'm getting closer to you each day

You make a way when there is no way

I used to shut you out, I was on my own

You were knocking at my door, but there's no one home

Never been good at this praying thing

So much on my mind, don't know what to say

I need you, Lord I'm real, and I hope that you see

That I know I need your love to come rescue me

And here, I give you my heart, please mend

I need a savior, I need a friend

That will never leave my side, in the storm and the rain

And comfort me and take away all my pain

Lord you came and you changed

My heart and you rearranged

The way I see you, and now I know for sure

My heart's been searching so long

With you is where I belong

Faith Fanatic

I've had to deal with things, and I've been in situations
That had me thinking, and it had me contemplating
What is my first, my second, my third, and my last resort
Is it wrapped up in things of this world, or is it with the Lord
His ways are not our ways, and we may not understand
And when the world thinks I'm down, that's when I going to stand
I got this peace, I got joy, I got this way about me
Folks that don't understand, got a lot to say about me
But it's ok, I'm going to fly straight
I don't need validation from you, to live my life my way
Going through the highways, and the byways
God said it ain't enough to preach, you need to live the right way
Living ain't living, until you're living with the Holy Spirit
Faith without works is dead, so you better get up, and get it
I want a faith that causes me to walk on water
I want a faith, that I can't help but talk about it
I want to move forward, don't want to lose ground, and
I want to build a faith, that can move mountains
But if you're living for the Lord, then expect a fight
Because in this walk, we walk by faith
We don't walk by our sight
Get that peace, that joy, that love, that passes all understanding
And when you fully get it, you'll become a faith fanatic
With the faith that I have, you can call me a faith fanatic

I'm going to stand, through my storm, my rain, my grief, my havoc

And it is my plan, to run to Jesus and to grab Him

Can't take my joy, because I'm a faith fanatic

Face to Face with Myself

Had a conversation in the mirror, face to face with myself

He said what's wrong with you dog, I said, nothing, I'm chasing after that wealth

I'm not tripping, you're slipping, I'm up on my grind

He said if you keep chasing that wealth, it will just be a figment in your mind

You need the Word, the scriptures, the books of the Bible

Money can't save you, but His Word is survival

I said who do you think you're talking too, I'm a gospel singer and writer

Sometimes I lace flow, and even unbelievers say it can't get no tighter

I'm sick with the word play, you're lacking in vision

I'm going to sing my way to the top, then I'll get my division

Division meaning prophets, prophets meaning ducats

So much money, I have to move it with wheelbarrows and buckets

Get my mom a new house, my dad a new whip

Take the fam on shopping sprees, get all they can get

It's the American dream, and I want my portion

People trying to stop me with distractions and distortion

He said boy you need to stop, go ahead and wave the white banner

Because you've committed suicide with your delusions of grandeur

You were put here to serve, not to become a fake boss

You would be highly favored if you were allowed to wash the plate that Jesus ate off

Pride comes before the fall, and you been falling for a minute

You're so low to the ground, you can take a roundhouse kick to the face, from a midget

You must've forgot, that's why I'm here to remind you

YOU were the sheep that went astray, Jesus came to find you

He bandaged you up, held you in His arms

Told you that He already met death, so you don't have to meet harm

He gave you a talent, He nurtured and grew it

Those big boy pants didn't fit right at first, but you grew into it

Made you a minister of music, taught you to write and play it

He gave you a melody and a mic, and He taught you to sing it

Gave you favor with the pen, and favor on the stage

When your music started it was like you just got let out of your cage

But now the Godly hunger is gone, it's the money you're fiending

If you ain't got my check, I…. AIN'T…. SINGING

You better thank God that He's God, because you just spit in His face

You deluded your ministry, took the fame over faith

It's a fearful thing to fall in the hands, of the living God who can speak one word and cancel your plans

I hope you see my message, stop messing God's name up

Get your big boy pants, and step your game up

If you feel yourself slipping, and needing some help

Come back for another one on one, face to face with yourself

Come to Him

I preach, and I teach, and I go to the streets

And I pray that you know why I do this

I'm laying down demons and stomping them out

Even Satan is calling me ruthless

I'm running so hard, that I ran out my shoes

Can't believe that I'm running around bootless

But the devil keeps talking, so I'm going to keep running

His day bout to end with him toothless

The mountains are high, and the valleys are low

So, I pray that you know where you're going

If you don't, and you find yourself down in a pit

Then remember God's door's always open

But we drink, and we smoke, and we're having the sex

And we use it to help coping

But God has a greater love, sitting and waiting

Just turn to Him, that's what He's hoping

Circumstances Lie

Life gets rough, but you have to remember
Your circumstances lie
See your circumstances with a spiritual eye
You'll see, you'll see
It's not so bad, it's not so tough
It'll make you think twice about giving up, yeah
Your circumstances lie
Feeling helpless in a dire situation
All logic says it's over, you've met your demise
See your circumstances with a spiritual eye
You'll see, you'll see
God's legion of angels surrounding you
Continue to walk in faith, Jesus will bring you through, yeah
Your circumstances lie

Change in Me

I can't really express how good my God has been to me
But I'll do my best to just try
Pray in Jesus name, with an open heart, on bended knee
He's the rule maker of my life
See the way that I carry myself, everything I do has changed
You're wondering what's wrong with me
And everything that I used to like, I don't like anymore, it's strange
But it's a good thing, can't you see
I love His shield of protection that covers me when I'm attacked
And I love the way that He changed my life, and I know I can't go back

In Love with Love

You Used to Love Him

Excuse me, beautiful

I know things just haven't been the same

Since he left, but girl I got you

Don't let him hold

He's just another selfish guy, with his eye on the prize

He can't hold you down, no more

So, take my hand, girl I'm strong

You can cry, all night long

Let him go, and I won't let you down

I know your heart it fragile

And I know just how to handle it with care

Let's go for a walk, by the water

I know you'll love it there

With the sunlight in your hair

Let my love take you away from here

And I know it's hard to bare

But I've been waiting so long

It's time you got right, you left that lame

I can show you what a real man is

Update, upgrade, elevate your game

I can tell by the look in your eye, that

You've been crying, allow me to dry that

Just forget about the things that he put you through

You can start over with a clean slate, just me and you

Take my hand, because I know

You used to love him, baby, you should stop debating

No, you shouldn't be chasing, you'll forget him

I know I might sound crazy

But you should be my lady

And start working on some babies

You used to love him, you'll forget him

Write A Song

You are all I want to do

I can't help but to think of you

You're my dream, won't you please come true

For me, baby

The more time that I spend with you

I'm falling deeper in love with you baby

You and I are like a Rubik's Cube

At first, we're complicated, but it then it gets easy

It's you and me, we're all alone

No one's around, we're in the quiet zone

I got my pen and pad, I got the music on

I just want to write a song

We're constantly going up and down

Sometimes we cuddle all day, some days you're not around

And it's in those times when I'm feeling down

I look to you for the words, but no words are found

How did you, escape my mind

And why would you, leave me in a time

When there's so much to say, but there's no words to find

The block is on, I got a writer's mind

The music makes me move

I'm falling right in the groove

I love it because it's so smooth

It's pulling out all the truth

In me, pen and a pad

And let me do something bad

Best lyrics you ever had baby

You are all I want to do

I can't help but to think of you

You're my dream, won't you please come true

For me, baby

When the Wind Blows

When the wind blows, where's it going, where's it been

Doesn't seem cold enough to be an arctic breeze

Definitely not warm enough to be a tropical breeze

Who was the last person this wind passed over

Was she beautiful, did it glide across her cheek

As if it was the gentle hand of the man of her dreams, whom she will never meet

Was the gust strong enough to blow away the tears of loneliness

Leaking from the windows to her soul

When she felt the wind, did it blow her hair back

Was she upset that the natural elements that engulf this world

Took it upon itself to take her salon manufactured style and turn it into a natural wonder

Did the wind blow her skirt up, as to give her an organic Marilyn Monroe experience

As the nameless wind filtered itself through her very existence

Wrapping her in a translucent and ever flowing comforter

In the midst of the howling wind, and the discontentment of her own heart

Is the pinnacle of what she's always wanted but will never find

And in that split second where she is caught in the glitch where sound doesn't exist

Did she think about me, the lips the were created and crafted exclusively for me

Did they formulate the three words that many long to hear, I love you

Did she place those words on the wind ever so delicately, and watch it cascade through the sky

Pierce through tree branches and continue off into the sunset

The wind is full of words, trying to reach their destination

It's full of emotions, too deep for words to comprehend

So, they just flow with an echoing whistle

It's full of secrets, some to be shared

Some to never be seen or heard from again

But if you listen, and if you look, the wind is full of stories

As it blows over a grassy field

Witness the natural rhythm exuding from each blade

Watch the giant tree as it sways back and forth

Like an outstretched arm crying out to God

Don't listen for the destruction, listen for the life

The howling of the wind, the moaning of a swaying tree

the clapping of the autumn leaves as the wind plucks them at the root

The earth has never been more alive

And if you listen hard enough, who knows

Maybe that "I love you" that was whispered across the world

Will appear on the horizon

And just as the winds settled

I looked up and gazed into the eyes of the last drop of sun and whispered

I love you too

TravelMancing

I really want to go to the Netherlands

Hike in the Polynesian Islands

Eat brunch in Southeast Asia

Margaritas on a beach in Jamaica

Swim in the oceans of Santorini

Wander the streets of Italy

Romancing in Vienna, showing chivalry

Imagine all the possibilities

Get lost in Spain

In Japan taking day trips on the bullet train

A night cap down in Fiji, they'll be glad I came

Slow dancing at night in the Maui rain

Go to Monte Carlo and sip Sangria

Hit a club down in Costa Rica

Fall in love with a fly senorita

Dinner in Brazil with Mamacita

Go shop over in London

See the castles down in Dublin

In Dubai drinking champagne, bubbling

Wouldn't that be something

Watch the sunrise in Budapest

Walk in the fountains of Croatia

Have a picnic in Iceland

Relax at a coffee shop in Malaysia

Spend Christmas in Vienna

Thanksgiving in Morocco

New Year's in New York

Then to Cabo for a taco

I want to quit the day to day

And visit place to place

Life can be shorter than you think

We don't have time to waste

Hands of Time

I got a lot to say, been holding in, where do we start

Been years of pain and hurting, tearing me apart

I can't write the feelings away, with a phrase or a remark

I miss my baby, I miss my high school sweetheart

I've cried about you, I've prayed about you

Lay awake about you, thinking of how I can find my way around you

And I dream about you, and I sing about you

Life is hard enough by itself, but it gets even harder when I think about being without you

It's crazy to think after all this time my heart still hurting

But it's plain to see that after all these years, girl you're still worth it

And I've never found a love like the love we shared, girl I want you

And there's nothing that I wouldn't do

I'd pack my bags and fly around the world for you baby

Miss Independent, but I'll wine and dine you like a lady

Just meet me in, Vienna, so that we can fall in love again

I'm sick for your love, you're the medicine

And you're the one that my doctor recommends

Our very first kiss was in a subway station, in Japan

Our very next kiss can be in Jamaica, on the sand

Make a stop, take a photo op, while we shop, and walking in Italy

Stick our feet in the blue sea, of the coral reef, while we're in the Florida Keys

We could easily

Hop a plane, and get lost in Spain

Slow dance in the Maui rain

Sun rises in Croatia, sun sets while in Malaysia

I'm willing to show you, just how much I will go through

If you just take my hand, and give me another dance

I know that we're not the same

We've grown, and we've changed

We don't ever talk to each other

But if we take one chance

All we need is one dance

We might remember that we love each other

Thinking back on all my regrets, you're always on my mind

Sex is so easy to get, but love is hard to find

Wish that I could rewind, turn back the hands of time

And go to when I was your baby, and you were mine

I'm The Kind of Guy You Need

We've known each other for some time

I have to tell you what's been on my mind

I know that your heart has been hurting for so long

But you don't have to be alone

I could tell when I first laid eyes on you

I wanted to take your hand, and be your man

Give you all the loving that your heart can stand

But I found myself waiting on you

Mending up your broken heart, when he was through

But it's ok, it's alright

I'm right here, I'll hold you in my arms

I'll shelter you from your nightmares

I've been waiting, for that smile

To smile at me

I've been patient, but oh so anxious

Watching you hurt, baby

Let me be your Dr., your love life's destiny

Girl believe me, I'm the kind of guy you need

I'm the kind of guy you need

I will treat you like my queen

Give you loving that your body needs

Just keep me in mind, I'll show you that I'm

The kind of guy, who will dry your eyes

I Like the Way

Baby, come lay it down

You're about to get the best of

I like the way you taste

What must I do to get that recipe

When I do, what I do

You say I'm taking your body to ecstasy

When you do, what you do

I feel like you're giving me your specialty

Slow it down, take my time

Making sure that I get it right

Talk French to your lower lips

Call that "wetting your appetite"

Tell me that there's breaking news

You have an exclusive, you want that mic

Then you say, daddy come lay down

Let me do that little thing you like

I like it, the way that you ride it

It's so worth it, I like the way that you work it

When you do me, I'm loving the things that you do to me

I like it, I want a taste, girl can I try it

I like the way, that your legs wrap around me when I'm hitting it right

I like the way, that you climb on top and ride it like a motor bike

I like the way, that you're working that ass like a nine to five

I like the way

I like it, baby

I Got It

We've been through the ups and downs

Ins and outs, round and round

But you always stayed down with me baby

And I know that without you, I wouldn't be where I am

I'm picturing you and me, in Italy

Let me rub your feet, run your bath, what do you need

I'll give you anything, because I'm your man

I'm working all day and night, working overtime

I'm on my grind, trying to fulfill this dream of mine

But behind every strong man, is a strong woman

I'm glad that you're on my team, I'm trying to do some bigger things

Take you to places, that you ain't never seen

Because I wouldn't be here, without you pushing

They say it ain't trickin if you got it

I guess it ain't trickin because I got it

And I promise, if I got it then you got it

Just let me know

If you need something babe

I promise, it ain't nothing babe

Just promise that you love me

Because I got it

Open Your Heart

I've been in love with you, for longer than you know
I know it's been so long, but I couldn't let it go
Wonder what it'd be like, if I saw you every day
So much that I would do, so much that I would say, like
I'm different now, I'm a grown man
Can I take you out, and dance to a slow jam
Can I cook for you, can I make you smile
Can we conversate, talk for a little while
Because it's no secret, that girl, you still have my heart
But I'm different now, and I want to know, can I have another start
I was young and stupid, and I took your love for granted
Now I'm living life without it, and girl I can't stand it
Open your heart, give me a chance
Allow me to be, a better man, to you
I want to get to know you, over and over again
I want to be your man, but first I want to be your friend
Hugging you, holding you, loving you, kissing you, missing you
Open your heart, give me a chance
Allow me to be, a better man, to you

Thought Process

Words

Sometimes I connect words, so poetically

Created from the exploding neurons in my brain

Traveling through my bloodstream, and exiting through my fingertips

Flowing smoother than the skin of a rose petal

Linking perfectly together like pieces to a jigsaw puzzle

Sentences and phrases that make longer strides than Usain Bolt

Paragraphs that cascade through adversity

Better than Michael Phelps, on the last lap

Statements and opinions that have the capability to shake you up, like Allen Iverson

Or leave you ran over, like the Beast Quake run

Stories that can turn your stomach

Worse than a scene from Saw IV

Tales that are taller than Davy Crockett, standing on his toes

On the shoulders of John Henry's blue ox

While I swear this to be the truth, I swear on a life

A life I secretly care less about than Donald Trump's hair manufacturer

That my statements are counted as fact

The truth is painfully obvious, yet your intrigue has been sparked

The juice that fills the container of your curiosity

Is leaking out of your pores

Now it is your personal business, to find out what I'll say next

I hate that I love the way that you hate to love what I do

Words can take you anywhere

From a happy place in life, to the darkest part of your inner most being

The words of a story can take you places you've never imagined
They can put you in the midst of the chaos at Normandy beach in 1944
They can make you fall in love with a person who doesn't exist
They can make you miss a place, in which you've never been
They can even make you understand what it's like to be black in America
Words, so powerful and so often abused
The Bible says life and death is in the power of the tongue
Choose your words carefully, choose them wisely
Creatively construct a parable that brings about a change
You never know who's listening

Welcome to My City

It's the 206, ain't no place as hot as this

Rolling through the city, with my top down, reminiscing

About the days, I grew up in the C.D.

Homegrown, town business, 26th and King Street

This is the city that made me, this is the city that raised me

This is the city that taught me to be a man, not in these streets acting crazy

I built up a hardigree, I built it as part of me

I ain't a hood dude, but I bet you ain't built as hard as me

Rolling through the South End, must've been '02

'89 Dodge van, but it fit the whole crew

RB, Cleveland, G Field, and FQ

School rivalry, but it was crazy, we were all cool

A summer day in the town, put the top down

Cruise around, bumping sound

Come on baby let's ride

Hop in the whip and, hit Ezell's for the good chicken

Sweet rolls, then hit the West, cruising Alki

Bumbershoot kicking it, Hoop Fest swishing it

Folklife, The Bite, Torchlight is so ridiculous

And if you're a real Central head, then you knew Rick

Ask him who built Garfield, and he said he did, with 2 bricks

Late night drive-in, Dick's burger on deck

Greasy fries, tartar sauce, milkshake ooh yes

Quincy, Cobain, Pearl Jam, and Kenny

History's extensive, and we can't forget about Jimmy

Griffey and Kemp, Payton and Lynch

The Beast Quake run was iconic

But what do I have to do to get my Sonics

We, we, we are, Sea, Sea, Seahawks

Seattle's Best and Starbucks are beefing

It's a green state, so we're legally out here chiefing

Back in the day, when I was young

Friday night used to be a skate party, meeting at TLC

Meet me at the Needle, you can be guest

Concert at the Show Box, then to Hemp Fest

Let's ride, through the west, and the central, and the south side

Genesee and Skyway, alright

Hit the Junction for the function, Pioneer Square, we'll be clubbing

All night

Welcome to my city

Treat Me Like

When I didn't have a car, you said "you better get on the bus"

When I didn't have food, you said "stop begging and manage your money better"

When I didn't have a home, you said "stay safe out there"

Now I have a big house

A convertible BMW car

A kitchen full of food

To everyone on their high horse that looked down on me when I was struggling

If you're ever hungry, you can eat at my table

I'll pick you up

Treat others how you want to be treated

Not how they may have treated you

That Guy

I don't think I will ever be "that guy"

That guy that can stop traffic, walk into a room and all the ladies stop and stare

Whisper to their friends about how good you look

I'm not confident at all, but I put up a persona that I am

Just to mask the fact that I'm not

I'm not going to lie, sometimes I be feeling myself

Turn my swag on and feel like I'm…. "that guy"

But those delusions of grandeur are quickly diluted with the truth

And I get a violent thrust back into reality

Once, I was REALLY into this girl, but I don't think she was into me

We were friends, and worked together

So, it's not like I could avoid her if I decided to shoot my shot, and missed

Nor would I want to, we had a genuine loving friendship

I'm no hater, if she doesn't want me, fine

A couple friends told me that they want to smash her

I don't throw salt on anyone's game

Do what you want

I don't measure up, I wish I did

But I'm never going be the best-looking guy in the room

Just fat black and ugly

The friend zone champion

Riding the Fade

I find myself bar stool hopping, pain pill popping

Feel my time is running low, I'm Armani wrist watching

Pain isn't stopping, I'm addicted to shopping

Question of the decade is, when's the next album dropping

The Ports aren't New, but I drag them with ease

Insomnia running rampant, I combat it with weed

Let me quote you a price, what you want from me

I'm not a battle rapper, so my style's not free

Life caught me with the fade, now I'm riding the wave

In the prison of my mind, just a free walking slave

When I started on this path, I was initially brave

Now I'm calculating, how much of myself I can save

You don't know enough to love me, but apparently enough to judge me

The hypocrisy in a smile, turns a beautiful gesture, ugly

Head dazed from the fade, while I'm riding this wave

Subliminal conscious, cautious yet consciously conjures every mistake I've never made

Take a second to wrap your mind around that phrase

Unbeknownst to myself, I purposely and purposefully

Dug up every right choice that I chose not to make

Like, if I would've done this, then maybe I wouldn't have gone there

Or, if I didn't say that, then maybe you'd still be here

All the should've, could've, would've scenarios doesn't change what I did

It doesn't change what it was, it doesn't change what it is

Look at it like this

If the situation was wrong, but you responded correctly

Does it exempt you from the consequence, no not exactly

Every action warrants a counter, every counter has a contingency

Every contingency has a backup, so every plan IS a conspiracy

Miss me with the theory, I'm weary, my heart's crying in pain

Blood dripping on my carpet, man, I know that'll stain

That's when I came back to my senses, I woke up in the end zone

She's breathing heavy, sweating, should've left her in the friend zone

I'm addicted to dicking birds, addicted to flipping verbs

I'm so addicted to dicking, it's like my name is a dick of a word

Addicted to cigarettes, addicted to sweaty sex

I'm overly addicted to my dick of a mindset

Addicted to buying things, addicted to smoking green

Addicted to contradicting myself, every time I sing

Complexity, divided by stupidity

Equals the number of times in a day, that I ask myself

Why

Understand, I just gave you a glimpse of my reality

Building still standing, but the framework's a travesty

Curtains look great, but the windows are getting mad at me

Brushed it up like a tooth, but in the back, there's a cavity

Fresh coat of paint, I'm confident when you pass me

The paint is just the makeup for some skin with bad acne

I keep my grass green, but it's really Astro Turf, and I'm not an athlete

The inside stares are too rickety to keep on climbing

Chandelier is made of QZ's, but I'm fronting like they're diamonds

At first glance the house is beautiful, but upon further inspection

You'll notice the foundation is cracked, and the house isn't even facing the right direction

Man, I can't believe the fade caught me

Who am I kidding, I keep the fade on me

It helps when getting lonely

Escape from reality, like that's my only homie

The irony is that, when I don't really want it on me

I brush it off like a hater, and instantly it's up off me

But then that begs the question

If I can avoid the fade, and keep it from round me

Then why am I always riding the fade, what's that say about me

Where Are the Words

What to write, what to say

Not much is popping into my head

I feel like the words to explain how I feel

Do in fact exist

This isn't some new monstrosity of a situation

That mankind has never encountered

I believe it is commonly referred to as writer's block

The words to sum up the deep thoughts, slamming against the walls of my heart

Are looming around the stratosphere

Orbiting like Russian satellites

It seems to me, that since I know they are out there

Riding the waves of forgetfulness on my brain

It shouldn't take more than a moment in time

To pluck them out, and put them on paper

Yet…. here I am

Without a single word to come to my aid

When words, delicately and poetically laced together

Is your only outlet

What are you to turn to, when they do not come flowing to your rescue

I'm at a loss, I have no answer

Nor do I have words

At this point, I guess it just isn't the appointed time

To say what is really on my heart

The day that I have the words necessary

To say what needs to be said

That my friend, will be great day, indeed

Peace and Chaos

It is in the silence where I find peace

Yet in the chaos is where the action happens

Peace for the mind, body, and spirit

Chaos for that hunger, that drive, that determination

Relaxation by the fire, with smooth jazz

Leading my mind to a serine oasis

The adrenalin of living each day to fullest

Because you may not be blessed with a tomorrow

Wrapped in a blanket of silence, I find peace

Amidst the chaos of my life, I find myself.... alive

Number Ones

June 29, 2009

It sounds cliché to say, but on that day, a piece of me died

I remember hearing the news, and I refused to believe it

I assumed that like every other problem you had, you would Beat It

The truth of the matter is that I seriously Rock With You

Your music made this Man In The Mirror do the moonwalk with you

For over half your life, I saw you fight the good fight

While the world was concerned about whether you're Black Or White

Nothing will ever come close to the original

You only found out Diana was Dirty, because of a Bad move, and transformed you to a Smooth Criminal

On that day, I had to stop and really think about

The Way You Make Me Feel

I got sad to my core, so I threw on the MJ highlight reel

Your music is amazing, your concert's a Thriller

To this day, I've yet to see music videos that are iller

Creatively, I feel you, I understand what you really mean

I've been where you've been, I got me a Billie Jean

You're a creative inspiration to me

One of the main reasons I never give up

I don't quit, I don't complain, I Don't Stop 'Til You Get Enough

You lived an amazing, inspiring, and rough life, but hopefully now the critics will stop bugging you

Though you may not have felt it when you were alive

On behalf of you true fans, I Can't Stop Loving You

Time goes on, and you see the change in things

Fall turns to Winter, and Winter turns to Spring

Music sounds different, men barely even sing

But one thing that will never change, the title of King

Hustle Like A Boss

You got the people who work, I call them the grinders
You got the people who leach off others, I call them the finders
You got the people who distract you, I call them the blinders
You got people who are haters, I call them the sidewinders
I'm a grinder, a worker, my hustle's immaculate
A man on a mission, that description is accurate
If laziness consumes you, I assume that you're lacking shit
Get rid of that part of your life, disinfect it and fracture it
My moves are as smooth as jazz, my hustle is as hard as rocks
My vision is clearer than Visine, I can change direction as quick as a fox
I can create something out of nothing, kind of like a magician
Dream it, create it, do it, that's how it comes to fruition
Always adding something new, I'm addicted to addition
Crunching numbers in my head like a mathematician
I'm not proud, or above any certain kind of work
I wear a suit to the office, then I change and go shovel dirt
Painting your house, or clean out your basement
Rake up all your leaves, then I sweep up the pavement
I'll clean out your gutters, clean the windows with Windex
You need some papers filed, I'll create you an index
You need a babysitter, all the kids love me
That's a lie, but at least my nieces will hug me
I can insulate your walls, I can move all your furniture
I can handle all your laundry, that's including the comforter

I go from walking the dog, to washing the car

I'm willing to work on any kind of jobs that there are

I'll scrub your kitchen floor, or sand your hallways

Any day's a work day, I like working all days

I'm a hustle-holic, I don't care what the birds say

If you need a song written, I'm sick with the word play

I never sold drugs, but I still got dollars

I never pimped a girl, but I still pop collars

I'm not a rubber band man, but I'm a low-key baller

Only 5'10 in stature, standing on my wallet, I'm taller

I never stole a car, but I'm pushing a drop top

In 6th grade, I was hustling Mambas and Pop Rocks

I keep my collar clean, so the law can't hurt me

I refuse to let any other sucka outwork me

I work too hard for my money, just to buy out the bar

Contrary to popular belief, I'M THE BIGGEST BOSS THAT YOU'VE SEEN THUS FAR

Drinks Up

I want to be one of the greatest

One of the ones, you want to listen to

And when you do, you are entertained

And pick up a jewel or two

Lyrics that cultivate your mind, and gets your blood pumping

People say they want to change, but all they ever do is nothing

Now's your opportunity, time to come up with something

But you shrivel up like a shrimp, like Bubba Gump is coming

I start conversation, hustle like a Jamaican

But they railroad my story, that's a Birth of a Nation

The government wipe their bloody hands on the same towel, and they plan to reuse it

Try and hold them accountable, they dismiss and excuse it

People ask why I go so hard, why do I do it

America's a time bomb, I have to defuse it

Whether rain, hail, sleet, snow, you're going to hear the best of me

But put your hands on me, and you're going to feel the rest of me

They're testing me, pressing me

Don't have no respect for me

But everything is A-OK homie, I'm blessed you see

Because absolutely nothing, is what everyone expects from me

So now I can roll low-key, I'm talking under your radar

Undercover Brother, I drive around in a plain car

Ok I'm lying, I drive a convertible BMW

If you've never ridden with your top down, then that sucks for you

But let me try to stay on topic, this isn't a subterfuge

Let me take you back to school, I fired the substitute

Understand that my wordplay is on another level

Metaphors so high, that I don't even see the devil

But like a music staff, I have the bass and the treble

Because I'm deep with it, to find me, you better get a shovel

So many different sides to me, more than the walls of an octagon

Schedule's crazy, I'm running around more than a soccer mom

I'm building a company, that produces books, music, a clothing line

And I have a 6 to 3, but I'm really working 6 to 9

I want to make you think, I'm talking about brain Pilates

How do you say you love the hood, while they're starving, and you push a Bugatti

What you mean black lives matter, you're shooting your shotty

You're tearing down an Enterprise, beam me up Scotty

I'm a mix between a psychological stimulator

Philosophical curator

A lightning bolt lyricist, the human defibrillator

It's bigger than rap, it's more than poems, it's deeper than that

The pressure is on, I feel the heat at my back

I got a platform and a voice, microphone and a choice

I give my gift as a present, Merry Christmas girls and boys

I'm nice with it, I'm about to spaz, check out this rhyme scheme

It might leave you speechless, have you doing that mime thing

Get on my team, this is my dream

It's a time thing, soon the whole world will be doing my thing

I have people sleeping on me, like when Portland skipped Durant and picked Oden in the draft

I have people hating on me, saying I should take my bars and throw them in the trash

I have people showing fake love, hyping me up, but I know its gas

And I have slick people trying go behind my back, like a no look Lonzo pass

I'm a Visionary, picturing things I don't even have yet

Card never declines, and never write a bad check

But then I watch the movie Belly, and ironically hear the sobering words of my man X

Yo, shut up, you ain't even put the weed in the bag yet

We're always eyeing, and spying, dying to try and skip the process

But the journey's how you learn the skills, to enter that contest

I got the best

Subliminal chemical, rhyme scheming ritual lyrics you heard in your life

What, you think that I'm kidding, then you must not be listening

I got the punchlines hitting harder than Ray Rice

It's show time when the cam's on, mice's on, band's on

I have adamantium lyrics, yours are softer than a tampon

You dust up, I dust off

You go around, I go across

You get hired, but I hired the boss

My lines are rough like a jagged edge, yours are baby butt soft

I have an unknown, undiscovered, crazy vernacular

Flipping words like pancakes, I'm a lyrical spatula

A lot of people swear they know me, but I don't even know half of you

But if I make you think, that's my goal, I couldn't be happier

I'm the plug, show me love

I'm blowing up, that's what's up

If you're on my team, then this is to you

Drinks up

Built Bad

Have you ever looked in the mirror

And think that the person looking back at you is entirely too ugly to be associated with

It's a really hard thing to come to grips

With the fact that you are an unfortunate looking person

"Real beauty's on the inside" is the famous quote that everyone has heard

But what if that's just something that ugly people say

I'm not here to judge your looks

I have absolutely no room to talk

My therapist once told me that I was crazy

I told her that I would need a second opinion

She said ok, you're ugly too

My advice, don't cheat yourself, treat yourself

If you're built bad, just be built bad and love yourself

72 Bars

First world conversation, America's debating

Who will be the next culture, to receive this hating

We're a walking contradiction, let me give the anecdote

You don't like her, but you take a picture for the cameo

Money over everything, it's all about the moola

Life's a celebration, Coronas in the cooler

They tried to give me Kraft cheese, but I turned it to Gouda

Tried to starve a fat boy, I had to get my food up

People think they know me, but there's more to my story though

I'm one up on you, mushroom in Super Mario

You can't leave the party though, until you get your cardio

Break a sweat while you're grooving, dancing to my audio

Peter was picking the patches, for the pickled peppers

Jason was jamming the Jordan Jump Man jelly's

Sammy's soul searching, because something said he will see why

But Eddie has no eyes, so everyday he's like Eli

I wonder if you'll be my, fly senorita

Bring the whip and caramel, part time barista

We can get a pizza, and listen to Aretha

It's cold outside, we can cuddle by the heater

In real life I'm quiet, bet you didn't know that

Bet you can't picture it, we can take a Kodak

We can pull out the fine China, sipping Cognac

I love it when you wear my T-shirt's and my throwbacks

Women stripping, and they're shaking what their mama gave them

More bucks, more butts, more motivation

Men aren't raising babies, only see them on occasion

Big Mama praying, saying that isn't how I raised them

Cash rules everything around me, hold up

God rules everything around me, so what

Even as a kid, I got respect when I rolled up

I pop, pop, pop out the can, soda

I guess at some point, everybody feels worthless

Start to wonder what you're doing here, what's your purpose

Your mind starts to go crazy, it's working like a circus

Now you're lying on a couch, paying for a service

You say you want to change, you say you want to stop that

So, you stop at the bar, and take a shot back

Chilling in your Manolo's, grubbing on some Rollo's

Every five seconds, need to stop and take a photo

Kids today don't respect the game, or the hustle

I'm trying to get it all and I will son, Russell

What do you know about Mayo sandwiches, the struggle

Routine traffic stop, ending in a tussle

Moving through life, using different tactics

Continental hopping, jumping around the atlas

Every single life has a timer, you have to manage

Dark skin brother, with a light skin advantage

Everyone wants to be the biggest and the hottest

But they quit, because they can't stomach all the losses

You no bar having, un-syncopated, syllables are hella basic sucka's

I'm familiar with the process

I advance, where you stall at

I fly, where you fall at

We both auditioned, I received the call back

And you're mad, because you saw that

Hating, because I'm all that

Trolling on the internet, nigga where the bars at

You're a Rook, I'm a Knight, see me in the day time

Yeah you got my Pawn, but my Bishop's on the same line

You say that you're a King dude, hold up, king who

Little homie you're lite work, I'll have my queen handle you

People used to tell me to my face, that I'm silly

I guess I changed really, or grew into the real me

Looking back on my past, I feel it should've killed me

God had to break me down, so he could rebuild me

Rebuilding a building, floor to the ceiling

It's a messy process, hammers and drilling

But when the dust settles, and your floors level

Take a look around, everything's looking so much better now

Now your boy's back, back right in front of you

Don't act like you know me, because I don't know none of you

Some of you can swerve, I'll kick it with some of you

As for the rest of you, I thank you for coming bruh

My Squad

What can I say about my little brother, man, dude is amazing

Honestly every day I look at him, and I get inspiration

Remember you were 4 years old, standing their reading

You were 4 years old, standing their preaching

I remember when I finally saved enough, for an engagement

I bought her the ring, I showed it to you

You said aww, in amazement

I had it all planned out, yeah, I knew what to do

Here you come running in the room

Yelling Mo, CJ got a ring for you

Hahaha, man, I'm going to always be here bro

And don't ever change who you are, because honestly you are my hero

I look up to you, I like what you do

Even told mom when I grow up, I want to be just like you

Home schooled, good grades

Curtain opens, you're center stage

You got a job, getting paid

Got into the baseball academy

Boy so smart, you can be what you want to be

Engineer, baseball, archeology

Don't press, just be what you're called to be

It's a trip, to think, you used to follow me

And now we here, side by side

You got a little peach fuzz, and we're seeing eye to eye

Believe me when I tell you, I'll ride for you

And I wouldn't think twice about dying for you

Because I love you J, brothers never part

Even when I leave this earth, you're still going to have my heart

Now, my favorite girl, my best friend

When I tell you my sister's my heart, believe me I ain't playing

Relationship is so tight, who'd a thought we'd have that

When the tears came down your face when I moved away

Man, who could plan that

The more that we seen, the more that we said, the more that we know

The older we get, the closer we get, the more that we grow

You're telling me things, I'm telling you things nobody knows

Welcome your kids to camp kill a kid, haha, inside joke

I was in 10th grade, you were in 12th, that's when we got cool

Family field trips to McDonald's, while we're skipping school

We used to argue and hate each other, get worked up

Look at us 20 years later, we're getting turned up

I remember the night, mom called me

You were in the hospital

I was trying to get there, trying to make moves

But I had a meltdown like a popsicle

There ain't enough time left, to fully say

Without the love of my sister, I wouldn't have my life today

Believe me when I tell you, I'll ride for you

And I wouldn't think twice about dying for you

I love you Meg, we'll never grow apart

Even when I leave this earth, you're still going to have my heart

I can't explain how much I love my squad

And you'll never have to fight alone, because I'll always stand tall

We're a squad, brought together by God

We're going hard, and I promise that you'll always have my heart

And I want to let you know, make sure that you know

That I love my squad

A Letter to My Father

My father is the kind of father that you wish you had

In no way is he perfect, but who wants that Leave It To Beaver dad

Yeah, my sister and I might've got jacked up once or twice

You know, that kind of whooping that made you think about life

People say it's wrong to spank your kids, and try to make father's the mean guy

We've been disciplined a lot, but.......did we die

He's a "go with the flow" kind of guy, does what he can, to make a situation work

When it's snowing, why spend money on gloves, when tube socks will work

Why make 3 Root Beer floats, when you can make 2, and just drink a quarter of both?

He never talked about why we should help people in need

Instead, he just showed me.

He dragged us to every volunteer event, I would be bored, my mind would roam

As a child, you don't see the importance of spending one morning a month

Singing to the residents at a retirement home.

No understanding on why you're feeding the homeless every week

But as a grown man, I can't imagine NOT giving back to the streets

He's not the nicest, he's not the meanest

He's not the tallest, he's not the leanest

He's not the messiest, he's not the neatest

He's not the strongest, he's not the weakest

He never had ALL the right answers, trust me...we knew that

And he farts a lot, but hey.... guys do that

He isn't the most sentimental, feelings can be weird sometimes

Sometimes he scared the life out of me, but I could see that my tears killed him inside

I know he did the best he could, with the hand he was dealt

And there was no shortage of discipline, whether it be a church shoe, hand, or belt

Though I couldn't see it then, I understand now

Staying out of trouble, your words AND belt taught me how

I'm all grown up now, with a life of my own

Yet you're still in my corner, helping me hold on

We've traveled, we've sang, even played racquet ball

We've talked, and we've fought, and every birthday, you call

They say we walk just alike, talk just alike

Even got the same swag when we rock upon the mic

Aside from our "hair growing" differences, and our clash on clothing, it is with all certainty that I can say, I am my father's child! When I grow up, I want to help my kids out when they need it, I want to go do karaoke with my son, I want my grandchildren to call me and ask to stay the night, I want to have my son's back and throw the first official punch in a fight at the Seahawks game lol. I don't know what the future holds for me, but you are still leaving me a great blueprint for being a great father. I love you dad, aka Kool Breeze

A Letter to My Mother

The older I get, the more I understand

The sacrifices you've made, changing your own plans

You put yourself last, in order to put us first

Did your best to shelter us, and tried to take the brunt of the hurt

I've grown up, you raised me, and I'm doing the best I can

I may not be rich yet, but you've raised a successful man

If God wrote your life into a symphony, you would be my favorite song

The world knows you as Super Woman, but I refer to you as Mom

I know I'm kind of outspoken, and I can get a little wild

But I live for those moments I make you proud, and you say, "That's MY child!!"

It's only right to say, you're the beginning of my world

I call you Mother, I call you Mom, I even call you my girl

Your beauty is scenic, smile like the sunrise

Eyes like the sunset, beauty illuminates like the moonlight

My Mother's a superhero, a gladiator in your presence

The stature of a monument, I look at her with reverence

She was the first line of defense, from the bullies on the playground

Momma don't play around, the bullies don't want to play now

She showed me love when she'd hold me, love when she'd scold me

She whooped my butt with a toy once, but she did it with love.... or so she told me

She encouraged my greatness, sent me around the world

She held me up after my first heartbreak, she understood how much I loved that girl

You stood by me, even when you knew I wrong

You always told me, but we end it with "I know you're grown"

And when I got locked up, in 03, I understood why had to send somebody else to get me

To see your baby on trial, for something he didn't even do

Can drive a mother insane, you just want your baby home with you

Mom....your love, is a fortress, inside of 8 tornados

Surrounded by tigers, bears, snipers, and about 90 halos'

"Oh, my goooosh" (in my Kevin Hart voice)

You are living proof, that God always makes the right choice

God must really love me, because He blessed me with you

Everything that I am, is because of you mom

I love you

PS: Per one of our many conversations, I'm going to need you to go ahead and let Megan know that you said I was your favorite child! Feel free to tell Josh too. Oh, and can you do me a favor and tell them to their faces, with me on speakerphone? I would love it if you described their faces! I'd much appreciate the story getting straight around here! It's about time the middle child started getting some respect around these parts! Much obliged! Good day Madame, I SAID GOOD DAY!!!

Letters to A Blind Man

These are the letters, to a blind man

Hate it or love it I'm speaking my mind

I'm at where I'm at, because I stayed on my grind

You're going to do this, going to do that

Laying all your plans out for me, but I don't have the time

I'm grinding, I'm hustling, making new moves

I'm breaking the records, I'm cutting new grooves

This a marathon, better lace up your shoes

I live my life, like I got nothing to lose

Oh, let me speed it up, moving like a cheetah cub

Let me get my hands on a beat, and I'll beat it up

A/C on CJ, because I'm heating up

Better hide your food, I'm starving, and I'll eat it up

Social media makes me sick, and I'm sick enough

People kill each other, they don't take it down quick enough

Cop sees a black man, protocol to stick him up

Letters to A Blind Man, that's my book, pick it up

These are the letters, to a blind man

I'm seeing a lot, but I'm saying so little

It's amping me up, but I'm trying to stay civil

The law says one, but the judge says triple

Need to watch out, keep your head on a swivel

The race isn't fair, but I run, I don't tire

Your pockets are deep, but my morals are higher

Say you spit the truth, but you Lucius Lion on your entire Empire

Vernacular on point, killing the game

Paint a story like a picture, give me a frame

Bars so heavy, need to lift it with cranes

I give my 2 cents, plus a dollar and change

Haters throw hate, hit me straight in the gut

Hide behind screens, while they chill in the cut

Eat this humble pie, while I'm whipping it up

Letters to A Blind Man, go pick it up

These are the letters, to a blind man

These are, the letters to a blind man

Every time I write a verse, I write it with my right hand

Feel It in America, all the way to Thailand

Lyrically drop a bomb, flashback Vietnam

Syllable crushing writing, is my business

God is so good, trust me, I am a witness

Don't know my name, and you're asking who is this

Tell them my name is CJ, that's who did this

Lyrically invincible, word play is critical

Speaking like a General, flow sick, it's clinical

I'm my biggest fan, some tell me that it's pitiful

But I recycle hate, I'm out here breaking down the minerals

Flow so sick, better get back

Breaking knowledge off, like it was a Kit-Kate

If you take one thing from this, Letters to A Blind Man, go ahead and get that